Some Scared Sister
Second Edition, 2025

©2025 by C.S. Mee. All rights reserved.

No part of this publication may be reproduced, distributed, or transmitted in any form or by any means, including photocopying, recording, or other electronic or mechanical methods, without the prior written permission of the author, except in the case of brief quotations embodied in critical reviews and certain other noncommercial uses permitted by copyright law.

This book is a work of fiction. All events and characters in this book are completely fictional. Any resemblance to actual people is entirely coincidental. All poems are the sole property of the author. Any resemblance to other published works is coincidental and not intended by the author.

The illustrations herein, crafted with care and love, used a variety of methods: physical drawing, digital drawing, collage & collaboration with digital & Ai tools (Dall-E, Topaz, Photoshop, Adobe Illustrator & InDesign)

No Ai was used in the creation of this writing.

ISBN: 979-8-9985315-1-4

Published by C.S. Mee, LLC

Printed in the United States of America

Some Scared Sister
C.S. Mee

Cover Art and Poem Illustrations by Anna Judd

CONTENTS

let's start here..1

when i fist wrote this, i wasn't sorry; now i am.......3

only incense & sad songs...............................4

the fog hovers above laguna's ocean head...............5

heavy..8

twenty-oh-five...9

sensation, explained..................................11

i understand how you hurt.............................12

fully realized..13

is it panic—or pain?..................................15

hey, mama...17

geese...19

nectar..20

nature, nurtured......................................21

some scared sister....................................23

blind...25

what would you call it?...............................26

letters from dad; greenlake, wi.......................27

just like mama........................29

when they called mid-night..................30

the monster my mother spoke of................31

what about the small things we leave undone when we die...33

hear me when i say......................35

l.p.//twenty-sixteen.....................37

don't wake........................38

(wo)man made.......................39

the protestant......................42

like ocean water......................43

mind, set........................44

can i be an artist now, daddy?................45

haven't felt it in a while..................46

a truth.........................47

class of twenty-oh-seven..................48

in motion........................49

twenty-eighteen.....................50

for the love of it.....................51

away, together......................53

let's end here......................55

mostly, these are for dad. the rest, they are for you.

i took time, and when i woke:

the air was clean, i could breathe, and i stood still

like a child, lone

in nature, blooming;

something new.

Foreword

...ck-memory haunts me. Blurs my past. Brick walls rise where there should be stories to retell, ...vies to peel apart.

...ause of this, I cannot tell you what happened, but I can tell you what it felt like.

...d a dream once; my husband held in front of me an old burgundy belt. He said he didn't ...ow how to tell me that I had once been silenced, told to quiet. In the dream, my husband said ...t all the women who had raised me were now downstairs, waiting to walk me through why I ...d been sentenced to such silence.

...the thing about dreams is that you must dissect them. Because there was no burgundy belt ...more of a whispered whip. There were no women but more of a call from myself. To see. To ...k for. To relive sensation. Like falling into the water of a warm tub.

...ide the searching, I found that my origin is my daddy; his origin: unknown. This book is my ...rt at cradling his fear in a way that doesn't coddle. This book is my way of saying, I did love ...ause I do understand.

...ile writing "Some Scared Sister", I placed pictures of my father on my walls for the first time. ...w, his invisible fingers shut doors in my home unexpectedly. Is that anger or an outcry, or ...ply a boy's attempt at touching the things that he could not face.

...is book exists alongside his aura in the ether; my ether.

...ese poems, for you, my reader, and for dad, they embody the power in pain, the crippling ...ect of abandonment, and the utter inevitability of loving a parent.

...ese poems are not answers and they are not questions. They simply are. Consider them art on ...ur wall. What do you see?

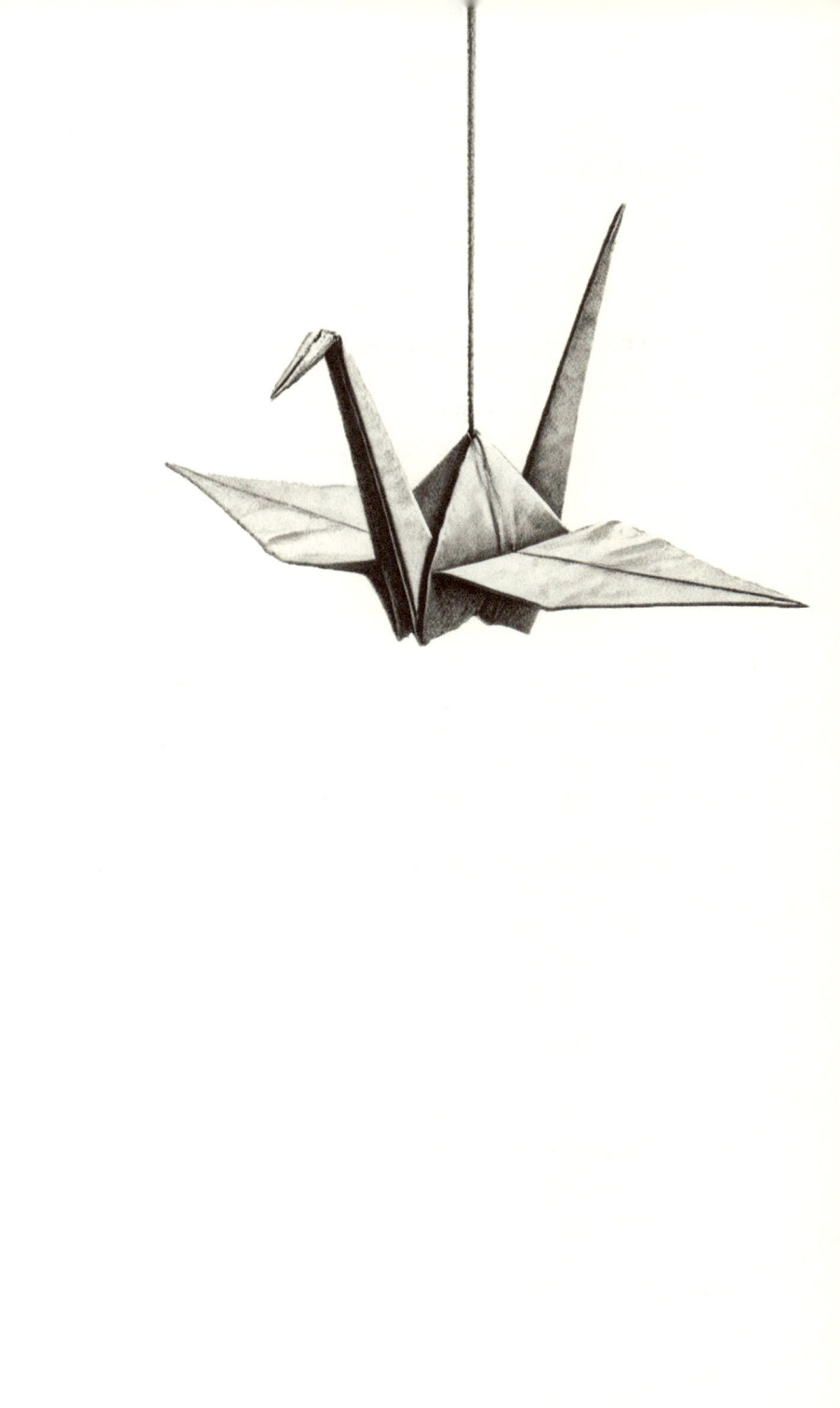

let's start here—

       with love:

       a little word with a large meaning— can it live
            unsettled,
                unsafe;
                    a blanket too short to cover cold feet at night—
   can love, the utter meaning of it, live inside a space that holds no honesty?

here's why i ask:

     because

i still don't know how i love you—
if it's innate, born with, or if
it's grounded in how you're gone;

maybe it's because there was some
tangible

    thing,

a piece of you i understood.

maybe loving a dad doesn't need to feel like the movies.

maybe it's simply:

watching tv together late night,
driving fast

      down

   steep beach city hills.

or maybe,

it's just: needing you nearby.
can you hear me now when i ask: what was it

you loved about me?

let's start there.

when i first wrote this, i wasn't sorry; now i am.

dad: i tossed all your letters, tore them from their envelopes and read them til
my heart went numb, i buried them
        under banana peels, beneath collected coffee grounds.

but you gotta know —

i got all the walmart cards, digested them, have your stories left to tell.

in your writings you taught me about god, how he might mend our wound.
truly, you said,
god would:

      find
            fix
                  fill us.

i tore it all up, ripped
your sentences in half, picked out
the letters from your words and peeled them apart,
placed them in a fire alongside the memory of you:

simply laughing
at sitcoms.

with time, you melted & molded:

a lone shadow amid a home far from me, ducks
the only song on a damp, solemn sunday night, small hints
      of tire hitting highway in the dim.

only incense & sad songs.

in twenty-oh-six, i lived in a room that wasn't mine and she held me like a mother. i grew inside of her with a lot of sadness— some honest teenage angst, but she gave me stillness and open space, allowed my mind to dance beyond closed doors, my body to collect air from shut windows. i know i will never breathe inside of her again, but she's here: at my finger-tips, with me as an entity, something i carry inside of my organs, a feeling i latch onto when i forget what an utter artist i can be. because when i listen closely to her reminders, i know that she came to me as an embrace, an audible breath of gifts, singing:

i see it, sweet child, you'll soar.

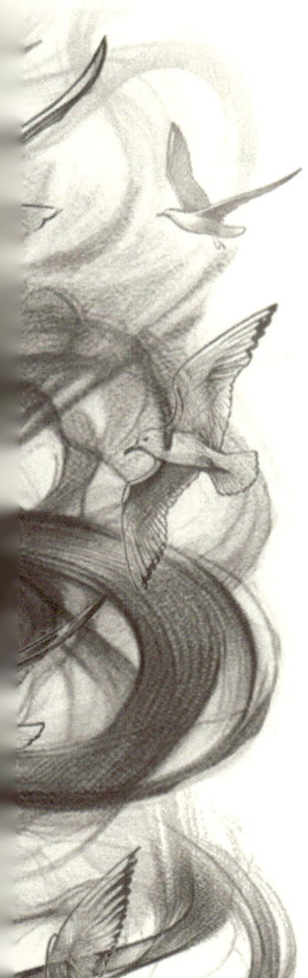

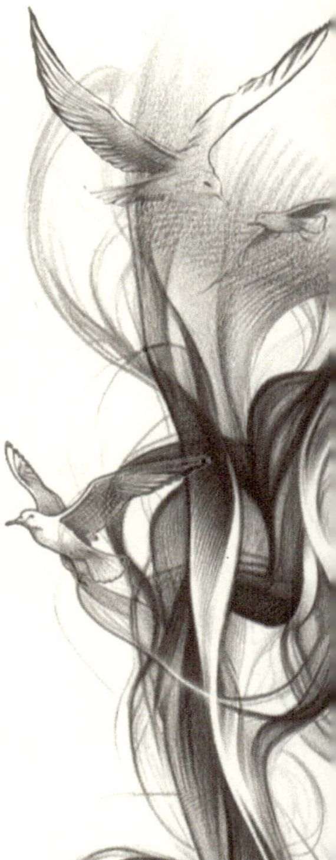

the fog hovers above laguna's ocean head,

and i wonder if my memory serves me:

      you were light-eyed and fair-chested, a shivering shadow reaching
      for warmth. did you love me or did i just have you covered; a blanket
      for all of your wrongs. me,
      a class ring; your achievement. i can hear you screaming:

"i created her, i must not be made of rot, she's of me and she shines;

look at her!

there's no need to fix all i've broken—

maybe,

      she'll

            fly

         for

               me."

heavy.

a soft breeze;
the air
      silk, its fingers
on my shoulders while i forget:
      you swooning while watching xena,
      that gaze of understanding me
      that you carried,

the moment i hit send—
on the message

      that held
      more words

than i can allow into memory.
the sentences
that simply,
without being simple at all,

      said:

dad, i'd like

      to no longer be near you.

twenty-oh-five.

what is it that i miss about little randall jones?
old spice at his neck,

    worn clothes
    wrought with holes, unwashed smells.

what is it that i crave about little randall jones?
sleeping on the bathroom floor,

    acne at his upper lip,
    the sour smell of worn out socks,
    hands calloused, and touching me.

what is it that i loved about little randall jones?

  warmth
  for no reason at all,

    other than, maybe,

he reminded me of what was no longer nearby:
floor beds, dirty clothes, cologne in volume; an unbothered energy amid a life
    unsolved.

sensation, explained.

not sure if i'm making this up since
you're gone now,
but something tells me we had an understanding;
a certain sense of humor,
our eyes catching,
seeing the same funky call-a-lawyer billboard on the highway,
some smeared lipstick on the mouth
of the fast food waitress. i don't
know exactly
because it's more of a feeling
rather than a moment i can retell,
nothing to relive,
just a warm-clothes-out-of-the-dryer feeling.
i've always wondered what it felt like to
love a dad. maybe,

that's it.

i understand how you hurt,

& how the feeling takes shelter; how it heats in your chest, finds its way to your inner organs, taps its finger-nails at your ribs & plucks pieces of muscle from your heart.

    but, i need to ask you this:
    are you tired, yet?

            truly, are you— tired, yet?

fully realized.

ever write the whole chapter while on a run, find the opening line in the shower, the ending at a red light?

yeah, all the time, i know.

here's what i say: the right ideas'll stick to your ribs, feed at your inner lining, fuel your next breath.

so, i say: don't worry about it.

i had four ideas last week that i can't seem to find today. but instead of pulling at my hair because i couldn't write them all down while i was soothing my son, feeding him his third meal of the day— i let them all lie; let the ideas i had lower themselves into the spaces they were meant to live, allowing them to blossom or wither as they must.

like this: i used to think dad was wreckage, a destructive disgrace, an utter layer of filth— when really, he was just

waning,
wilting,
wavering without will.

so, what was the idea that made it to the page, that sucked at my inner organs?

      loss;

loss of his life well-lived, loss of sincere, sober solitude, a willingness to just: be.

for to thrive would have been a stiff-
spined back-bend for him—

and he didn't need to tell me this, the idea had already birthed within me, the idea of dad, soaking itself into my taste buds, like how my hair feels between my fingertips. sensation, they call it.

the idea that he was a violent shadow, a tormenting dark place, was replaced with someone incapable of making a morning meal; he was merely:

sans guarantee.

is it panic— or pain?

not sure how you feel it, but for me:

i'm bleeding while healing, plummeting while pulling myself up, vomit one last time;

be still.

then: let your brain go black; disappear, rid the memory,

    sink while the water fills the tub.

you ever wake shaking; an hour-long sweat's run your body, crawl's all you got, cold porcelain tub's the only way to save you? you vomit, piss; remember to try & forget. you shake, rattle, sweat some more. feel
the hot water on your face, breathe, and don't look for solutions—

because planning,

    she's an enabler.

hey, mama.

don't lose me;
just listen:
your anger's an entity
(i know).
all the guilt,
it takes shelter,
(i know).
but listen:
it's
pain

        disguised

as exhaustion—

cus when i clutch the edges
of a porcelain tub,
i can only repeat
scribbled memories,
turn them

over,

    over,

        over.

like some movie, there's
hands high
in the air,
a voice loud—
words i've never heard.

like some novel, there's
fists heavy

at a door,
hard on wood—
emotions i've never felt.

this energy,
it claims
without reason,
it reads
like a borrowed book—

makes you want to sleep,
(i know).
but listen:
there's your story,
there's dad's,
    mine,
then

        there's a truth—

geese.

when i think i'll love someone, i picture us dancing:

carpeted floors or tile linoleum beneath our toes,
a pavement, hot against the soles of our runners;
we'd enter a sauntering of sorts, move
to some happy beat,
feel closer,
together like friends.

i just try to feel like friends—

nectar.

sometimes i kick the wrong rock and i'm down, knees bleeding, a teen, tongue-tied
and taunting, watching the rain as incense turns to ash, ears burning from hot head
phones blaring coldplay's 'a rush of blood to the head.'

was i wrong to hide in my room for all of those years? because, now, look at me—
i miss her. the hum of
the floor heater, coarse journal paper tearing from worn-out erasers,

waiting on a phone call from someone i'd never love.

here's the thing, and i'm sure you've felt it:
the older i get, the more parts of me i have left to miss. today i ache for her:
sixteen in a dusty bedroom, blinds open, mid rain, something angsty to say.

nature, nurtured.

i'm in love with the damned,

the damaged way out,

    the drink til i can't,

the inhale til i see black—

    it's in my blood,
    it's how

they have all carried themselves before me;

    be

        fore

            me—

some scared sister

not sure if you know but i got a lotta sad in me. it's a state i work hard to destroy, a place in me i wish i could teach a lesson, a piece i wish i could talk to, tell her to quit. but she's got her grip on my gut, nails in my neck—

and she's holding me like some scared sister,
fueled by failure,
torn apart by success.

here's the thing: dad was sad. very sad and all the time. about almost anything, everything. swapped dinner for meds, missed showers (in the end).

once he sat at the edge of a hotel bed, stared at a white wall while i lay restless, filling my head with how free it'd feel to leave him lone.

now: i let him live on inside of me, harbor space sans rent.

(family will carry us, wear us like worn-out sweaters when we pass. don't you think? ever felt it?).

i feel the fear in that

as i hold my son, sweep thru his gold curls, know:
they're dad's.

what parts of dad does my boy carry; what parts of dad will he always hold?

will they be sad?

or will they be full, filled with quiet, fond, pieces owned

but never shown?

blind.

what do you want from me? peace
and quiet wakings in the night? not sure
i can handle the harmony quite yet.
what's that you say? take it easy?
easy, what's that? are you ok, you ask. no,
my mind's spinning, you see, like a goddamn
ferris wheel; there's fierce fire, like bombs let off,

watch them drop—

what would you call it?

i could have easily been an addict like dad,
piles of pills, hard liquor, no courage.
instead i inhaled myself so no one could see

me sleeping for whole days, spoon-
ing yogurt from bowls between naps, leav-
ing granola bags by the bed as i'd turn-
in for the weekend—

most nights, i'd steal mom's wine, drink it from a yellow rimmed coffee cup,
chat with strangers on-
line

and cry hard at the top of the stairs—

letters from dad; green lake, wi.

i found you insane, talking
of nonsensical things: a new address again, faux reasons for not
holding jobs; a new faith and i think
you mention a dog. once
you wrote
of a lake swarming with ducks, a lonely home
sur-
rounded by red-
wood.

just like mama.

i'm working the clock
like dogs, leaving prints
where i land & it's like this:

life feels heavy when you rest,
all that energy & memory hanging ar-
ound you
like clouds.
it's an unspoken fury
in my bones & i'm spinning,

       leaving crumbs
where my agony speaks,
leaving clues
where i've refused
to heal—

when they called mid-night—

                to say
they'd found you,
i sat up in bed, uttered
a silent agony that woke my heart.
i crawled to the bathroom, met the edge of the tub
where i fell into
an inner cry so intangible, no one could hear me.

now,
on the memorial podium,
i'm projecting
in hopes
you can hear me,
feel my agony be-
tween your finger-tips;
as if you could access the tangible.
as if it all were,
what they call:

        sensation.

the monster my mother spoke of—

was manic and emotional, unable
to stand; he never

meant what he said.

he'd:
cover his eyes,
lie
about how he loved.

i'd say, mommy, don't look,
because the monster, she lives
in your home,
eats at your table,

    asks for help
        with her homework.

i'd say, mommy, i look
at the monster,
her eyes ever-green in my mirror,

and she lies,
about who she loves.

mommy, i say,
she shows me:

the water bed on fire,
floral dishes, broken in the sink;
mold, growing in the shower.

she shows me: herself
and how she lives

so fearfully

(inside of me).

what about the small things we leave undone when we die?

the hair clogging the sink,
macaroni salad in the fridge;
a printed photo on your counter
laying next to an empty frame—

hear me when i say:

how long have we worn this, daddy?
this inner scare,
the rustle & the round-
about;
the fear & the fall-
ing over
and over.
the burning in our
brains, begging
us to quit.

what if you'd learned to transform this
into art. i ask:
did you ever just try
to transform this
into art?

because i wonder what you
would have created if you'd
just transformed—

& i wonder
if you should've been a photographer,
taking photos of dirty public restrooms or elevator doors that can't seem to close. what
if you could write prose poems,
place them beside photos of: my children sad on saturday morning, our family's estate
sale on 4th and warner,
the way jack's shoulder rise, & shift, when he's trying not to cry.

& i wonder
if you still could, if it's still plausible, possible (what would be sensible— for someone
who's gone?)

i wonder:

if you had your own film based on your own lonely stories,

who'd be there

waiting,

    willing

        to witness—

l.p. // twenty-sixteen.

rose-prick red, my lips see the hand in your hair
as you walk at me through the alleyway. then: applying lipstick, (yours, a bit berry,
bright), you smile, eyes down, away,
then at me (nervous). i'm lifted, because maybe: we're the same.
at the party:
we hide together in corners,
palms rubbing carpeted walls of an old theater venue.
then, our eyes darting towards:
the man in green, his slacks tight and high-watered,
the woman in leather smoking
parliaments at the entrance. we blot our lips (the same),
pull combs from purses both black,
fix our skirts (the same). i almost miss it when:
we're far from the theater and no one's watching,
you wipe your mouth clean (nervous),
bright berry smeared on the top of your wrist. i almost miss it when:
i wake mid morning, my lips still rose-prick red,
your sentences in my mind, once full of gifts,
now humming,

lonely as a voicemail.

don't wake.

in my dreams,
you're speaking to me—

"i want my work to be:
intrusive, to capture
your attention, speak
fiercely.

i would paint

       out

             loud,

use strokes

to create noise, build
momentum."

in my dreams,
i sing back to you—

"you can.
just—

create, simply, for
the creator latching to your organs,

because she's screaming
and she needs you to know

there's utter promises and discovery
and joy when you just

make.

(wo)man made.

there's a branch growing (inside of me),

    she's thin,

        & she's leafless,

           & she's breaking (me)

                down.

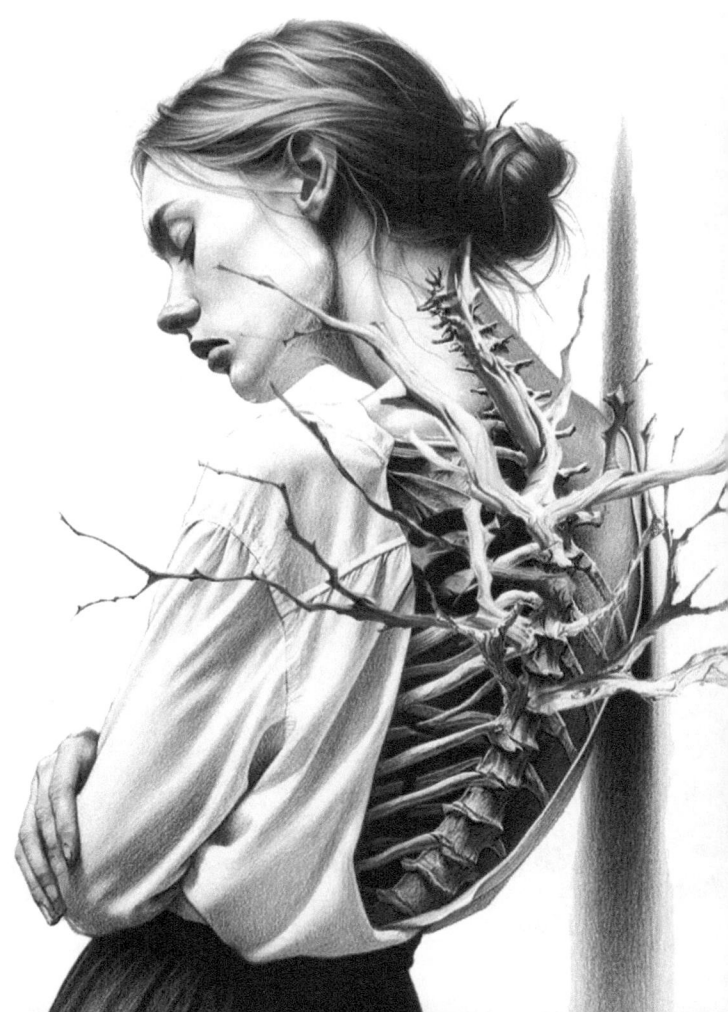

the protestant.

i know:
if i play someone else,
besides me,
then we can be:

some choir girl
and her daddy.

and they
won't see:
the gloss in your stare,
the high in your eyes; that
you'll never be

        born again—

like ocean water.

i wrestle with love
but it rests.
the past,
it stays put—
and there's power in that.
all of yesterday quiets and sets
itself down on a shelf,
settling into this library of lessons.
and as if filed away,
love lets
and lets—
itself

    be read.

mind, set.

there can be
so much noise a-
round what wrenches us,
what we wish
would peel away.
but if we
stop,
breathe,
notice (the geese flying south,
the warm wind at night,
a glance back at a friend
as she leaves),
then we can simply be
and let love lead
palms forward.
feel the quickening? it's

an utter shake into joy.

can i be an artist now, daddy?

can i get behind the wheel,
turn the tapes up loud,
use my vocals
to harmonize
in alto?

i can feel your brain burning,
but just listen:

if you'd let me
i'd be an artist,
and i'd take care of it,

inhale it as if it were so,
devour it

       entirely,

make it my identity.

oh, an artist: who could she be?!

tireless, effortless and lone; meandering only amongst
her masterpiece—

       she must be!

how lovely.

daddy, don't you think that's lovely?

haven't felt it in a while:

the ache. haven't sweat in some time:
the anguish. instead:

the swish in my stomach finds room to roam, finds
blankets to keep itself warm. the difference:
it's given a name. and it's never:
the utter unknown.

a truth.

i think, daddy,
if you wrote poetry,

you'd write
poems about people you'd always known: school girls in floral parachute skirts, your wife with braids in her hair, your mother stirring pasta, barefoot, in the kitchen.

& other times, you'd write
poems about people you'd never met: a businessman roadside, hands in his tangled hair, the lady in blue, delivering the mail, all that sad in her eyes.

then, a lot of times you'd write
poems about people who have never existed: your neighbor with the broken picket fence, the military widow who couldn't love you; your new york friend who stopped calling.

you could make it a game,
fill the lines with fantasy, then memoir, allow a lie, then sprinkle in the truth; let it all be read and read and read until it's understood:

> sometimes you need to lie to tell the truth.

class of twenty-oh-seven.

when we're young, teens— we seek identity with eager fingers—easily casting ourselves artists, living inside the mold, enveloping our bodies with the word (artist) and what it means—to be expressive, to wear our hair longer or shorter, to walk around with a pen in our pockets, a paint brush in every room. but as we age, and we become engineers and mechanics and office dwellers (something we never dreamed), the cameras leave our necks and they move to dusted desktops, our hands barely tapping the keyboard, and with that, we forget:

    we're all artists still.

in motion.

new friend,
let's dance
like geese in the sky,
frolic like fawn newly born.
i'm wondering what it would feel like if we fell fast
from a tall cliff,
landing like ribbons in the ocean,
loose and easy, invited.
i've always been: afraid
of the height
yet lately
i've been flying, jumping,
the sky selecting me,

    catching me as i soar.

twenty-eighteen.

    look

        out,

see how the waves wash the earth, how the sky touches tips of bird's beaks. do you see how this feels
like love lifting into the air when trees
meet sand, the rocks at our feet.

    look

        up,

see how the earth captures us here in this brilliant embrace. such honesty
the world will bring

when we just:

        notice.

for the love of it.

my body settles with your touch, a soft truth uttering promises like: i'll hold your shoulders in a pew at your father's funeral, take your burdens with me when i walk out the door. the other day i was speaking with a man who said his wife had always dreamed her husband would hold her as she slept. he responded by asking how he'd ever rest. last week i woke with the moon, was met with a familiar numbing in my chest, so i sat on the soles of my feet, knees to the bed. while resting, you reached for me, kept one flattened palm at my back, our free hands clasped tightly at my collarbone. and i thought, to be held at night is actually:

    the only way to rest.

away, together.

the waters wait with us,
their garden of glimmering
sea listening
to our breath-beaconed bodies,
the way we rustle with boots in the gravel, the wandering eyes of the wind watching the
gallant gifting
of our souls to its ocean. this is a moment fully realized, a lingering light of guidance, a
memory that will envelop us
as we fall favor to its saving song.

i find myself at the shore, cleansing
fear with found time.
i'm there
to collect,
cradle, and
cause joy.
i'm there to hold harmony,
to lather it with ability, and,

      see that?

  it grows—

what's the word
for the explosions
in your chest,
those hot heated vibrations.
oh such joy,
discover it,
peel
it
apart
with your fingers,

dive
into
it
head first—
    jump.

let's end here—

what do i want to say,

about how it now feels
to wake in the morning,

my mind alert and ready;
legs alive and twitching.

what do i want to say about the love affair i've had with the elements, with my poems, and with that book i read about the girl lost in the water,

or what about the love affair with my —self;
i should think on it.

what would i tell myself about the times i said no or the ways i sang yes.

last month, i jumped with my back to the water, a view of the big sur mountains the whole way down, my hands grasping for rock, trying to pull myself back up. but the rocks, they released, and they fell with me as i allowed my way down, towards the ocean.

and as i surrendered, i felt myself fall in loosely, feet scaled, fins awakened— gills at my temple,

now able to breathe,

off land.

Acknowledgements

This book would not exist without love. I send love back to:

My Husband. Who believed in me while I wrote in the dark. Who said. Do it right. Do it well. Do it every day. My Son. Who reminded me that being a child is to embody innocence. Who reminded me why loving a parent is without control. My Editor, My Artist; My Ideal Reader, Anna Judd. Who understood my work as if it were her own. Who understood. Who taught me that to leap for art, is to leap for yourself. My Therapist. Who, without, I would not have healed. Who, without, I would not have found the courage, or the words, to finish this book. My Mother. Who has always read my journals. Who encouraged me to be an artist. Who encouraged me. My Grandmother. Who always knew I'd become a writer. Who read my work, then asked me questions. Who read my work. My Step-Father. Who loved me, from my beginning, despite my blood. Who raised me, from my beginning, despite his blood. Who taught me that some trees grow purple flowers.

And My Father. Who loved me. Who kept my photos on his wall until his final sleep beneath them. Who tried to take my hand. Who tried. My Father, a mystery, and yet—

not a mystery at all.

About the Author

C.S. Mee emerges as a vibrant new voice in poetry and fiction from Southern California. As a wife and mother, her life is richly woven into her words, transforming personal struggles with anxiety and childhood memories into compelling narratives. Her debut, "Some Scared Sister," marks the exciting launch of her literary journey, promising a future bright with emotional depth and resonant storytelling. With a voice both unique and universal, Mee is an author who not only writes to understand her own story but also to resonate with the hearts of others.

csmeewrites.com

www.ingramcontent.com/pod-product-compliance
Lightning Source LLC
Chambersburg PA
CBHW030448100526
44580CB00002B/37